THIS BOOK BELONGS TO

For Mom and Dad

SALLY DENG

SKYWARD

THE STORY OF FEMALE PILOTS IN WWII

FLYING EYE BOOKS

LONDON | NEW YORK

C★NTENTS

★★★★★★★★★★★★★★★★★★★★★★★★★★

★★★★★★★★★★★★★★★★★★★★★★★★★★

FIRST FLIGHT

★

Three girls looked to the sky and wondered what it must feel like to be up so high. What would it be like to cut through clouds so swiftly that the wind struggled to keep up? How close to the sun could they get before its rays turned their vision white? They looked at a plane and decided to find out. They were going to fly.

The year was 1927 and it was an unusually warm day in San Francisco. The city felt sluggish and slightly uncomfortable. Hazel, however, was bursting with energy. She had come with her father to the local airfield as they did every Saturday. They 'ooohed' and 'aaahed' as planes swooped down, landing and crossing the runway. Today a pilot noticed Hazel's excitement and invited her to take a closer look at his aircraft.

"A Curtiss Jenny," Hazel whispered. She approached the plane slowly, mouth slightly open as she took in the sight before her. She reached up with both arms to touch the belly of the plane. The surface felt smooth and warm under her skin as she stood on her toes to reach the wing. When the engine roared to life, it was so loud that Hazel felt the vibrations travel through her body and rumble in her chest. She clenched her jaw to keep her teeth from rattling. Something clicked in her and she knew she had found her true calling in the skies.

"Baba, I'm going to fly this one day," she told her father.

Her father nodded. "I wouldn't be able to stop you if I tried."

Across the ocean, Marlene was reading under her favorite tree outside her home in the English countryside. She was enjoying the rare sunshine when, out of nowhere, she felt a tremor in the air.

BZZZZZZzzzzzzzzzzzzzzzzzzzzZZZzzz. It grew louder and louder and louder. Left, right, behind, all around. Where was it coming from? Finally, she looked up. Even from afar, she knew that mischievous grin all too well. She watched as her brother landed the plane on the field.

"Marlene! Hop in!" he shouted, waving his arms wildly.

"With you? In that?"

"What? Too scared?"

Marlene hopped in.

"Oh," she gasped.

Just a few hours before supper, on the outskirts of a small town in Russia, a foreign object sputtered and groaned across the sunset until it was forced to land in a dusty field. Lilya and her friends were immediately at the scene, clambering over one another like eager little ducklings trying to take a closer look. A man in strange clothes stepped out of the plane and their squeals of delight only grew louder.

"What is this?"

"What is that?"

"What are you?"

Lilya shuffled and squeezed her way to the front to look at the fallen machine. A low grumble and hiss could be heard coming from the inside. The small trail of smoke rising up caused her nose to wrinkle and her eyes to water. How had it been flying only minutes before?

"Are you a fairy?" she asked the stranger.

The man threw back his head and laughed.

"No, I am a pilot."

That night, Lilya showed her family her drawings of the aircraft.

"I am going to be a pilot!" she declared.

"I thought you were going to be a doctor?" her sister asked.

"Yes," her mama added fondly. "Lilya will become the best there is. She will take care of mama, papa and her brother and sister."

"Don't you have to be smart?" asked her brother. "All this little girl does is draw in her little book."

"I will be a doctor after I become a pilot."

"Don't be a fool," her brother sneered. "How will the daughter of a farmer ever be such a thing? Only in your dreams."

And dream she did. In her slumber, Lilya imagined herself,
light as a feather, bouncing across the clouds. During the day,
the image of the aircraft crossing the pink sky kept appearing
in her mind. Her room soon became littered with her renditions
of the memory. She was never satisfied with the results, though.
She knew that she would need to fly.

Throughout the years, the girls' passion continued to grow. With her brother's teaching, Marlene was the first to learn to fly. Up in the sky, it was only her and the elements. The harsh wind whipped mercilessly, leaving her parched cheeks a deep red and transforming her hair into a wild mess of knotted vines. Dense, smoky clouds enshrouded her and curious birds were the only witnesses to the daredevil glint in her eyes. Marlene earned her pilot's license before she even started driving.

When she finally found work, Hazel began her lessons. Money was still hard to come by and there were weeks when she was forced to stay grounded. During those days, Hazel read numerous books about the science of flying. When she struggled to understand some of the mechanics, her father was always glad to help.

Lilya, on the other hand, kept it all from her family. With only the slightest hesitation, she secretly joined a local flying club when she was still in school. She paid for her flight time by working extra shifts at a factory. Her mama and papa only learned of her hobby right before her 18th birthday. "They've asked me to become an instructor!" she exclaimed, her eyebrows scrunched up in disbelief.

CHANGE

★

In 1939, another great war began...

Hazel, Marlene, and Lilya braced themselves every day for increasingly worse news. From her daily papers, Marlene read about Hitler's rise to power and his invasion of Poland. Hazel found herself in heated discussions with those who were against allowing Jewish refugees into the US. Every night, Lilya and her family gathered around the radio to listen to updates about the rising tension between the Soviet Union and Nazi Germany. A heavy silence settled between their family and friends whenever word was received of fatal bombings and nonstop gunfire. The future seemed bleak.

Marlene watched as many of her male colleagues were drafted to help fight in the war. Wives, sisters, friends and mothers from Lilya's small town looked to one another and asked the same question:

"What can I do to help?" So they began working, each woman contributing what she could. Hazel watched as the women in her neighborhood took up all kinds of jobs: making rivets, sewing parachutes, nursing soldiers, operating radios, painting posters, repairing machines, driving trucks and much, much more.

Pilots like Hazel, Marlene, and Lilya wanted to help too. "Let us fly!" they pleaded with the government. But their cries fell on deaf ears. The girls huffed in frustration as those in charge laughed at the idea of women flying in the military. As the war continued, it soon became apparent that there were not enough male pilots to go around. The military's need for them soon became desperate. Women persisted, pointing out that the idea wasn't so ridiculous any more. It was necessary.

The call to join the Women Airforce Service Pilots, or WASP, was announced. Hazel's dream had come true. The US government was starting a women's aviation unit headed by record breaking pilot, Jackie "Speed Queen" Cochran. Although a civilian group, they would take on all the same tasks performed by the army's pilots. Still, whenever Hazel entertained the idea of registering, her palms instantly turned clammy. She confided in her friend, Elizabeth, who also felt the same.

"A Chinese American and an African American wanting to join? They will think us crazy and laugh in our faces."

"I've lost track of the number of times someone's laughed at my face. I'd rather they not spit at me, though."

They sat together in silence, imagining the worst-case scenarios.

"The sky shouldn't be limited to one color," Elizabeth said after a moment. "If we don't try, we'll regret it for the rest of our lives."

So they did. Apart from a slight delay, Hazel's amazing flight record qualified her for training. Elizabeth, however, was turned away immediately. Recruitment was very direct about why she was rejected. In fact, they soon heard of others like Elizabeth who were dismissed based on the color of their skin.

"What a waste of talent," Elizabeth sighed.

Hazel couldn't agree more. Unfortunately, segregation did not end in the US until more than 20 years later. It would be another 10 years after that before female pilots could officially join the military.

Bessie Coleman

Back in Great Britain, Marlene was brewing her morning tea when she heard:

"MARLEEEEEEEEEEEEEEENNNNEEEE!"

Her brother came tumbling into the kitchen, nearly tripping over his feet, and shouted "Look!". He held up the morning post and shoved it in front of her. She could smell the ink still drying from the press.

"Have you heard of Pauline Gower?" he panted.

"Have I heard of her? She's only one of the first women to get a commercial pilot's license. And she only started her own air taxi service," Marlene replied, slightly offended. "If you're interrupting my morning just to—"

"She's recruited eight women for the Air Transport Auxiliary!"

"The ATA? I thought they only took old or handicapped men?"

"Well, now they're apparently taking women!" her brother said with unmistakable glee. He spread his arms out as if he himself were about to take off. "What do you say, my dear sister? You think they'll take you?"

Marlene flipped her hair. "I can't imagine why they wouldn't," she said with a smirk.

As soon as she logged in the required amount of flight time, Marlene applied to the ATA. During the physical, her leg bounced up and down impatiently as she waited for her turn. She huffed as they fumbled over her flight and medical records. When the doctor pointed out something "funny" in her file for the third time, it was all Marlene could do to keep from pulling her hair out.

"Something tells me these army doctors aren't that familiar with the female body," she whispered to the other hopeful recruits.

When she was finally given a clean bill of health, it took all of Marlene's remaining self-control to keep from laughing out of pure joy and relief.

Like many of her friends, Lilya wrote letters to Colonel Marina Raskova, the most famous aviatrix in the Soviet Union, asking to be given the chance to fly in the war. She was not expecting to receive a telegram from the colonel herself.

"Bring suitable clothing. If selected for training you will not be returning home."

Lilya frantically started packing. Her mama laughed when she saw the summer dresses in her suitcase and replaced them with woolen leggings and a heavy coat. She also found a doll under her sketchbook.

"You are a woman now. You should not bring a doll to war," she said to her daughter before taking it out.

That night, she gave Lilya a necklace. "For luck."

Lilya's family managed to scrounge up the money to send her to Moscow. The entire length of the train she was in had been strafed by enemy fighter planes just days before. She tried her best to keep warm as freezing air whistled through the shattered windows and bullet holes. Lilya had never been to a big city – Moscow might as well have been a fantasy land from her childhood stories. The buildings loomed over her, blocking out the stars with their imposing height. The subways rumbled and rattled underground and echoes of screeching metal bounced through the cement tunnels.

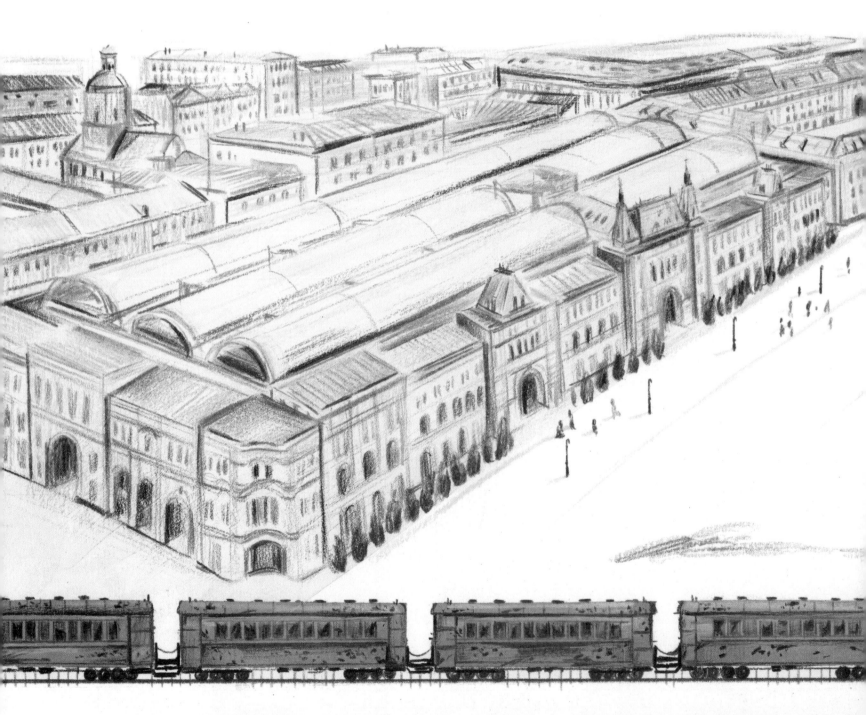

When Lilya finally arrived at her interview, she was surprised to be greeted by Marina Raskova herself. She was sitting across from her idol, the woman who had flown nearly four thousand miles from Moscow to Komsomolsk and broken the long-distance world record for female aviators. She knows my name! Lilya kept thinking. It was very difficult not to pinch herself. When the interview ended, she almost didn't realize that she had been accepted into the program. She was going to start immediately! She started to say thank you but her words struggled to escape the tightness in her throat. The colonel smiled and gave her a cough drop.

JUST LIKE THE MILITARY

★

By 1942, all three girls had been relocated for training. Hazel's new home was an airbase in Texas. It was extremely daunting arriving at Avenger Field in Sweetwater. People in powerful positions wanted the WASP program to fail. "You're taking all the jobs from our men!" they said. Nearby residents kept their children inside, convinced that the ladies were going to be crashing planes left and right.

Marlene was stationed at Hamble airfield, one of the few all-female ferry pools in England. She made sure her makeup was applied evenly, her hair curled perfectly and her posture ramrod straight. Despite her attempts to look professional, male ATA pilots still whistled and catcalled at her whenever they showed up. Instead of turning a deaf ear to their rude remarks, Marlene would coolly glare at them until they retreated. She did not have time for their foolishness.

Lilya transferred to Engels, a port city in Russia. Trainees were housed in a cowshed that had the stale smell of its previous tenants. The creaking wooden walls did little for preserving warmth; Lilya had never been more grateful for her mama's help in packing. Everyone was exhausted from their travels, but sleep did not come easily as they whispered excitedly with one another about the coming days.

They were given their flying gear… but it was all too big.

Lilya and her friends put their sewing skills to good use, and stuffed discarded magazines into their large, man-sized boots.

"My, don't we all look fetching?" said Marlene as she
and her fellow ATA pilots tried on their official uniforms.

In their humid barracks on the other side of the world, Hazel and
her friends had to coordinate and purchase matching outfits.

Their days consisted of endless marches, military exercises, nonstop drills and challenging courses, from early morning until late at night. They sang songs to make the mundane tasks pass by more quickly.

The moment they sat in a pilot's seat made it all worthwhile. There were so many different types of aircrafts! Hazel started out learning with primary trainer planes like the PT-13D and gradually moved to combat planes used by the army. Marlene preferred flying the single-seat fighter aircrafts, especially the Spitfire. It was incredibly fast and always gave a particular kick at takeoff. Lilya also had to master flying in the dark of the night. In no time, they were comfortable performing different acrobatics and landings.

Marlene wrote letters but the censors blacked out whole paragraphs to keep information classified.

"I just want to know what's happening back home!" she vented to her new friends.

The ATA was an international program and pilots from all over the world had joined. Always a lively place, it was common to hear more than one language spoken at the same time.

"I feel like I'm living in a television story," Marlene observed.

"But without all that troublesome drama about finding a 'good marriage'," laughed her friend Anna.

They spent their days off riding the train to London and dancing the night away.

Hazel's bay mates also enjoyed spending nights out
at the local bar. She had to stuff pillows under her friends'
blankets to make it seem as if they had not broken curfew.

When their room became too suffocating and humid, they dragged their
beds outside and slept under the Texas stars. Her father sent a constant supply
of books and aviation magazines. On clear nights, Hazel liked bringing one
out to read under the moonlight.

"Read to us too!" her friends would say.

Sketching helped Lilya through some of the tougher times. One day they had to cut their hair short like a boy's and every single trainee wept at the loss.

"Oh Lilya, your beautiful hair!" her friend Tatyana cried.

Some of the girls kept a lock of their hair in an envelope or between the pages of a book. That night, Lilya and Tatyana stayed up late handing out small drawings and writing poetry to lighten everyone's spirits.

There was always a high chance of someone failing and washing out. Hazel and her bay mates reminded one another to double check their faulty flight equipment. When the homesickness overtook Marlene, she would seek out her friend Anna, whose willingness to offer kind words was endless. Lilya was supposed to follow military regulations and address everyone by last names. But the trainees all laughed at the forced formality and only complied whenever a male officer was around. Through their shared hardships, the girls formed deep bonds with one another and were able to keep pushing forward. They knew their goal was almost within reach.

IF A GIRL COULD DO IT

Then the day arrived. After months of intense training,
the girls officially graduated. They were ready.

Their celebrations were cut short by the urgency of war.
They immediately started work. One of Hazel's first jobs as a WASP
pilot was to ferry planes. This meant she flew across the country to
deliver planes to different bases. It was not unusual to be bundled
up in her leather jacket at the start of the flight only to have stripped
down to her basic flight suit when arriving on the opposite coast.

She came to appreciate flying at night. When the moon was
full, it lit the way for her. If she couldn't get to a secure base, she had
to land and guard the plane all night with a .45 automatic pistol.
She had come a long way from simply flying a Curtiss Jenny.

Hazel also performed flight tests on some hastily repaired or haphazardly-put-together aircrafts. Many male pilots refused to risk their lives ferrying these planes so it was up to the ladies to deliver them. Hazel once had to make an emergency landing because oil was leaking from one of these repaired planes. As she was wiping down the windshield with her blouse, a ruddy-faced farmer came charging toward her.

"A SPY! A JAPANESE SPY!"

She was detained by the local sheriff until her commander got on the phone to demand they let her go.

Another job assigned to Hazel was to tow targets.
A long banner would be tied to her plane and she would
fly around as male soldiers on the ground practiced firing
anti-aircraft guns at her. With real bullets.

PTHROOMMMmm

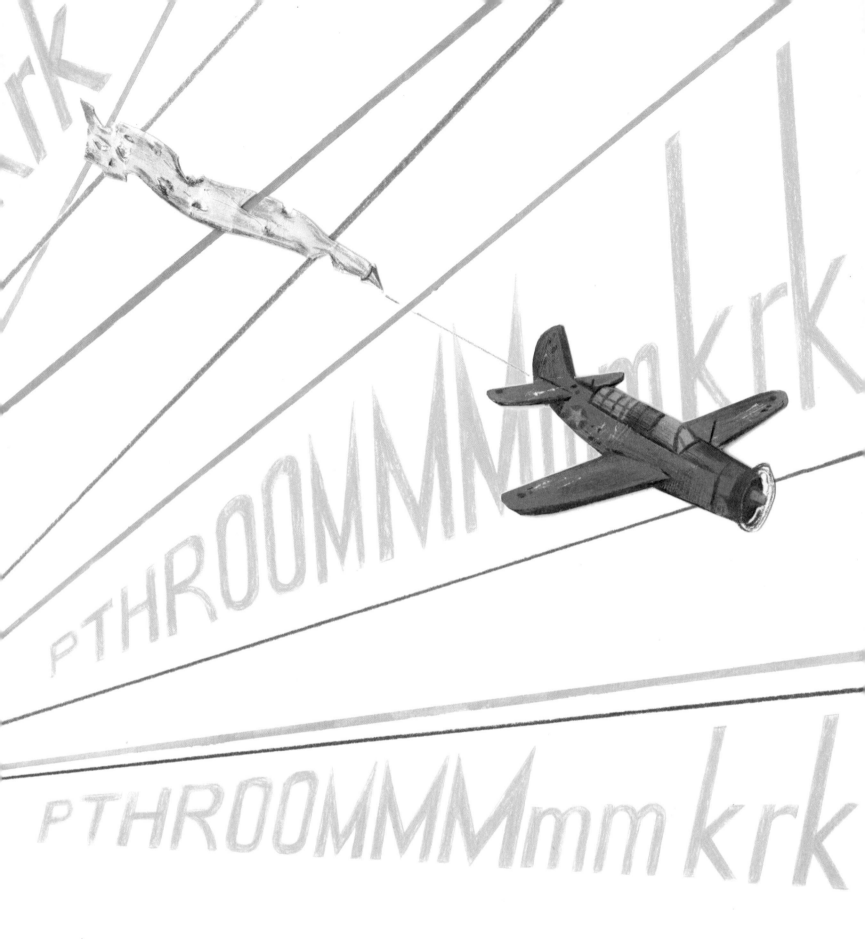

Hazel counted the bullet holes afterwards.

"Wow, that one was close," a crew member pointed out.

Marlene's main job was also to ferry planes. English weather was erratic and fickle; clear mornings quickly became foggy afternoons. Radio silence had to be maintained for security reasons, and barrage balloons dotted the skies. She also helped transport refugees and patients to hospitals. ATA pilots were never forced to fly in bad weather, but Marlene and her friends refused to be grounded. They completed four to five flights a day – putting off even one day of assignments would cause a great setback.

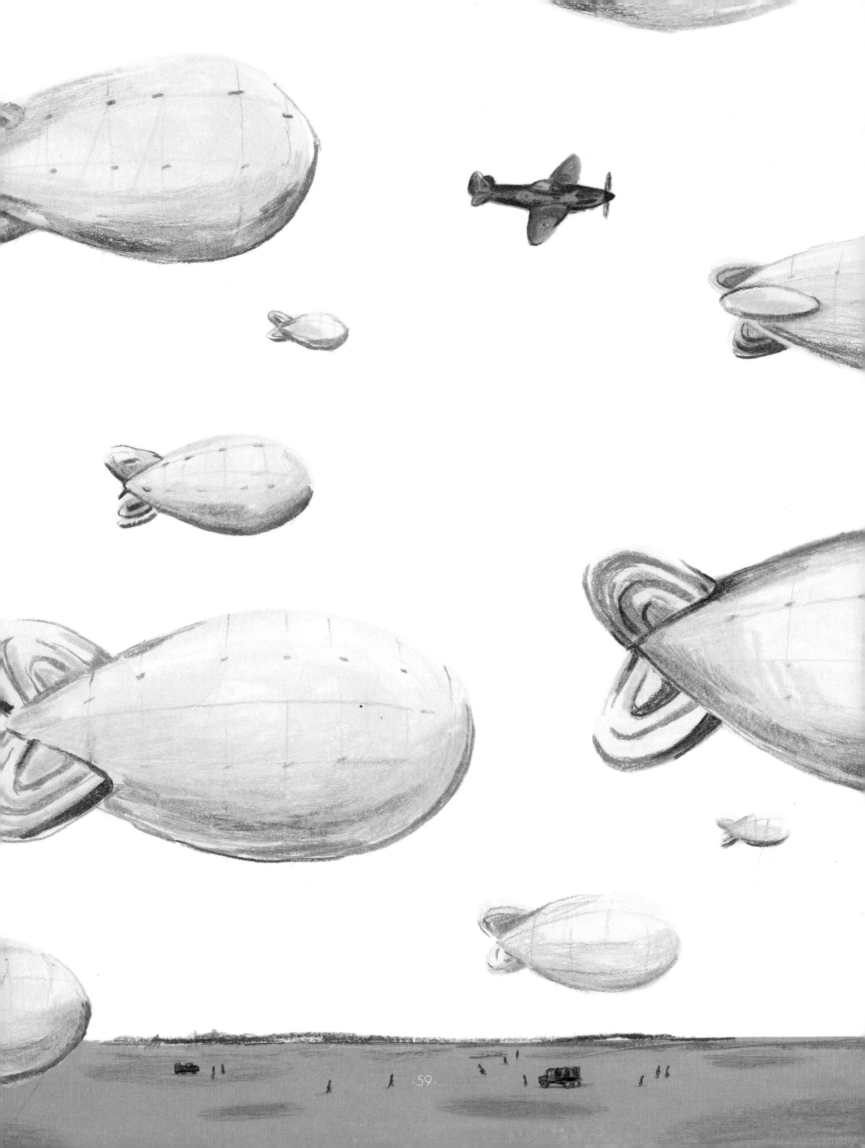

On an especially bad day, a blanket of fog prevented
Marlene from seeing a high cable. She began descending
when her plane hit the line, did a cartwheel and…

CRSSshhmKkpph

She somehow walked away with only a bruise.

There were also risks in being so close to the enemies. She was transporting a lieutenant when Marlene noticed a slight movement out of the corner of her eye. It was a German plane. She stayed calm and quickly maneuvered herself out of machine gun range. By the time she looked back, the plane had disappeared in the clouds.

"What a way to start the morning, right?"

When she received no response, Marlene chanced a quick glance back at the lieutenant. The look on his face resembled her brother's when, as a child, he had fallen off a tree and snapped his wrist.

"I didn't know it was possible to turn that pale," Marlene mused to herself.

Lilya was assigned to the all-female 588th regiment, whose sole purpose was to fly combat missions against the Germans. In fact, they were the only female combat regiment in the entire world. Lilya was ecstatic. She was going to fly for her country! Some of the ladies were disappointed when they were chosen to be mechanics, commanders, or navigators instead. Tatyana was assigned as Lilya's navigator.

"I may not be a pilot, but I will be in the air with you." Lilya was grateful for having Tatyana as a friend.

The 588th regiment's mission consisted of heading towards enemy lines and performing aerial raids at night. Lilya and her friends constantly moved around. If they were lucky, they would sleep in local villagers' homes. Unlike the ATA and WASP pilots who flew a number of different planes, the 588th was assigned to fly only one plane: the PO-2. Known as the "Mule", it was made entirely of wood and was quite slow. During the day, the entire crew had to push the planes closer to their targets. Lilya helped carry bombs and fuel by hand when the trucks were stopped by muddy fields. Sometimes they had to go back and push the trucks. Despite all this, they still found time to take up embroidery. Lilya would write to her mother, asking for threads in every color of the rainbow.

When the sun set, the dangerous part of their mission would begin. Pilots and their navigators climbed into their PO-2s. Lilya sat in front, Tatyana in her own seat behind her. Each team followed the same plan. They would fly out to the enemy line and get as close to the German camps as possible. Before they got into hearing range, Lilya would shut off the engine and glide her plane down towards the target. *wsssssssssssssssssssshhhhhhh*

The thunderous wind in her ears was a whisper to those on the ground. When they were close enough, she pulled a lever that would drop bombs down below. If the lever became stuck, Tatyana would stand up and push the bombs out by hand.

"Night Witches!" Horrified cries rang out from the enemies on the ground. They flew back to their airfield to refuel and repeat the whole process again. Missions began at nightfall and ended at dawn. The crew hardly slept, but this way, neither did the Nazi soldiers. The most she and Tatyana ever flew were 18 trips back and forth in one night. Afterwards, Lilya counted 38 bullet holes in her plane. She kissed the necklace her mother gave her.

Journalists and photographers tried to interview the ladies at every opportunity.

"The public wants to know you!" they shouted.

Hazel and Lilya avoided interactions with them by ducking out of sight or mumbling an excuse and quickly running off. Marlene was more blunt. Once, after climbing out of the Hurricane she had just delivered, a few members of the press were able to catch up and crowd around her. She gave them a tight smile.

"I'm sorry gentlemen, but I have very important tasks to do," she said as she shouldered past them.

There was no time to worry about what the reporters wrote or what photos they took. There was always more work to be done.

THE FLIGHTS AFTER

No matter how much time and dedication they put into their jobs and no matter how flawlessly they performed, there were still those who couldn't accept the idea of a female pilot. Critics wrote articles about how they were unfit for a man's job. Ground crew members would check the cockpit of Hazel's plane, asking: "Where's the actual pilot, sweetie?"

There was always a double standard. After an especially exhausting flight, Marlene was greeted by the lieutenant waiting for her. He frowned when he saw her disheveled hair and smudged mascara.

"I was told that a beautiful young lady was bringing me a P-51 Mustang," he said. "What happened to her?"

The ladies never felt ashamed of themselves.
As Lilya's band of friends would say:
"We are women and we're proud of it!"

The hardest days were the ones when they would lose a pilot. They'd become so close that it felt like losing a sister. When the government refused to pay for funerals, Hazel and other WASPs started a pool of funds to help. Lilya came to truly understand the meaning of loss on her first mission. As she was refueling, she was informed that one of their planes had been shot down by enemy fire. Just like that, two of her friends were gone. It felt as if an iron weight had suddenly dropped onto her chest. The world had gone quiet and all she could hear were the echoes of her own heartbeat.

"Lilya, we have to keep going!" Tatyana pleaded, shaking her shoulders desperately. Lilya felt herself nod. She struggled to fight off the shakiness in her limbs as she climbed back into the Mule.

Everyone had stories of close calls and Marlene knew that sooner or later, someone's luck was going to run out. It still came as a shock, though, as her eyes fell on Anna's name written neatly on the notice board where the dead were posted. Blinking back tears, she slowly walked to the bathroom and locked herself in a booth. She gave herself five minutes to remember all the moments when Anna had comforted her and cheered her up. Afterwards, she wiped her tears, reapplied her makeup, and stepped out to start her day's work.

Despite these difficulties, Hazel, Marlene, and Lilya committed years of their lives to their missions and their passion.

"A part of me wants the War to continue forever," Hazel confided to a friend. "When will there ever be another chance to fly like this?"

When the War finally ended in 1945, it was bittersweet. With it came the end of terrible battles but also the end of their careers working for the military. They knew the government would not feel the need to hire female pilots any more. How would future jobs ever match up to what they'd experienced?

Even knowing all this, the girls pushed themselves to the limit. Hazel ended up piloting over 78 different types of aircrafts before the WASP program was abruptly ended. She never once refused to fly a plane, no matter how notorious it was for breaking down or catching fire. Marlene delivered almost 1,000 airplanes as an ATA pilot. She learned to fly many of these planes by consulting her flight manual just minutes before she climbed into the cockpit. Lilya flew over 800 missions with Tatyana in the 588th regiment. Every night she would set aside her own fears and anxiety and dive headfirst into danger.

Without knowing it, pilots like Hazel, Marlene, and Lilya were paving a new path for young girls in the generations to come. They proved to everyone that women could be amazing pilots. They were three girls who had looked to the skies and wanted to know what it felt like to be up so high. With little to no recognition and very little pay, they jumped at the chance to do what they loved most.

And we are so grateful they did.

AUTHOR'S NOTE

This book began with me coming across a black and white photo of Hazel Ying Lee standing proudly in front of a plane in her pilot outfit. My first reaction was "Wait, Chinese American women were allowed to be pilots back then?" Three years later, after hours of research into the critical roles they played in WWII, I am still in awe of these amazing women who flew for their own countries. If you have the time, please please *please* go read more about them.

✷ ✷ ✷ ✷ ✷ ✷ ✷ ✷ ✷ ✷ ✷ ✷ ✷ ✷ ✷ ✷

BIBLIOGRAPHY

Nathan, Amy, and Eileen Collins. *Yankee Doodle Gals: Women Pilots of World War II.* 2013.

Williams, Vera S. *WASPs: Women Airforce Service Pilots of World War II.* 1994.

Whittell, Giles. *Spitfire Women of World War II.* Harper Perennial. 2008.

Keil, Sally Van Wagenen. *Those Wonderful Women in Their Flying Machines: The Unknown Heroines Of World War II.* 1979.

Noggle, Ann. *A Dance with Death: Soviet Airwomen in World War II.* 2001.

Myles, Bruce. *Night Witches: The Amazing Story Of Russia's Women Pilots in World War II.* 1990

ISBN: 978-1-911171-88-1

Order from www.flyingeyebooks.com

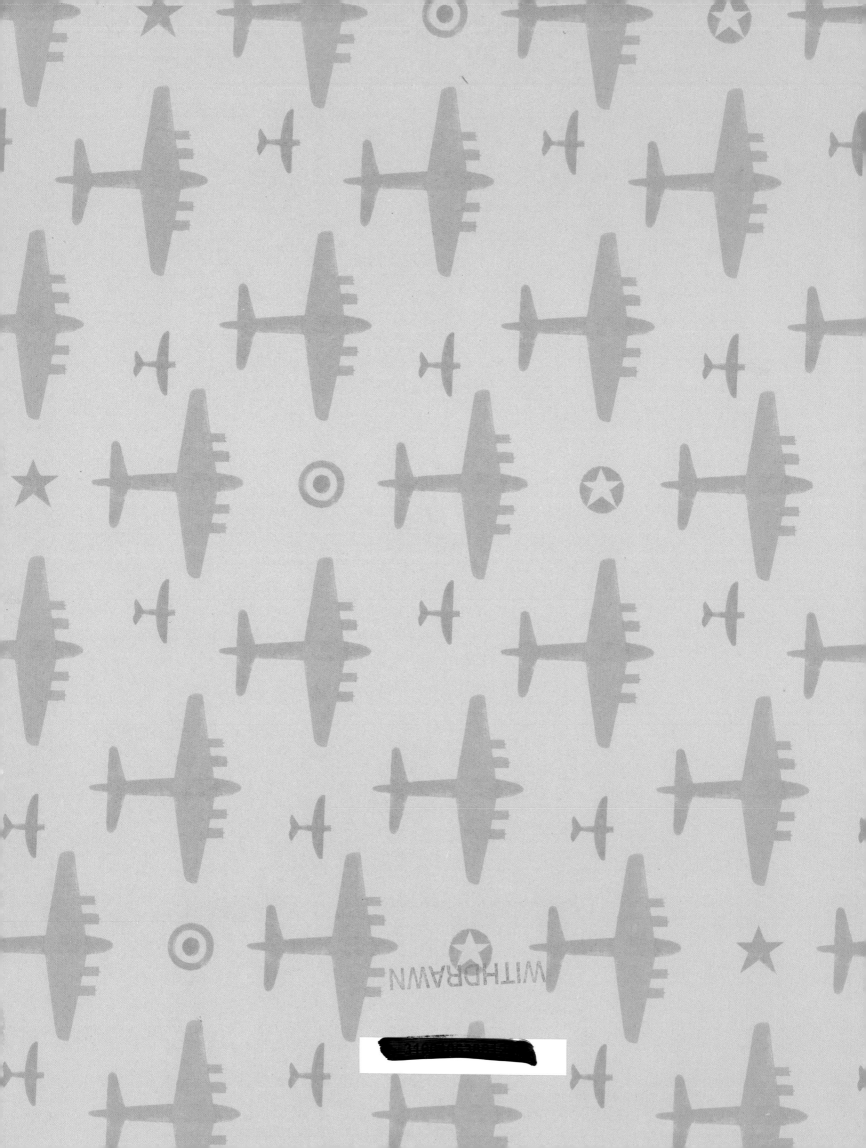